Animals in the Water

Written by Jo Windsor

PEARSON

T0360103

Look at the fish.

The fish are
in the water.

Look at the birds.

The birds are
in the water.

Look at the snake.
The snake is in the water.

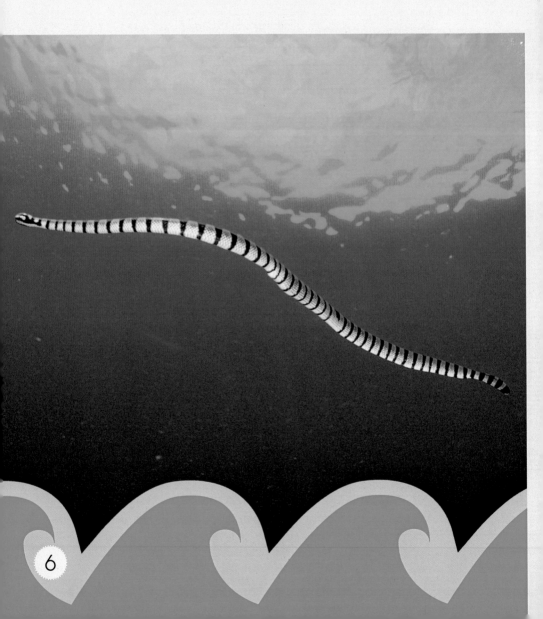

Look at the hippopotamus.
The hippopotamus is
in the water.

Look at the shark.

The shark is
in the water.

Look at
the penguins.

The penguins are
in the water, too.

Look at
the penguin.

The penguin is
up on the water.

Index

▬▬ Guide Notes

Title: Animals in the Water
Stage: Early (1) – Red

Genre: Non-fiction (Expository)
Approach: Guided Reading
Processes: Thinking Critically, Exploring Language, Processing Information
Written and Visual Focus: Photographs (static images), Index
Word Count: 72

THINKING CRITICALLY
(sample questions)
* What do you think this book is going to tell us?
* Look at the title and read it to the children.
* Ask the children what they know about animals in the water.
* Focus the children's attention on the Index. Ask: "What are you going to find out about in this book?"
* Why do you think the birds go into the water?
* Why do you think the snake is in the water?
* Why do you think the penguin is up on the water?

EXPLORING LANGUAGE

Terminology
Title, cover, photographs, author, photographers

Vocabulary
Interest words: fish, water, birds, snake, hippopotamus, shark, penguins
High-frequency words: too, up
Positional words: in, on, up

Print Conventions
Capital letter for sentence beginnings, full stops, comma